Geography Zone: Landforms™

Exploring

PENINSULAS

Melody S. Mis

PowerKiDS press.

New York

To Lillian, Jeff, Jeffrey, Blake & Devon Riber

Published in 2009 by The Rosen Publishing Group, Inc.
29 East 21st Street, New York, NY 10010

First Edition

Editor: Nicole Pristash
Book Design: Julio Gil
Photo Researcher: Jessica Gerweck

Photo Credits: Cover © Heinrich van den Berg/Getty Images; pp. 5, 9, 13, 17, 19, 21 Shutterstock.com; p. 7 © National Geographic/Getty Images; p. 11 © iStockphoto.com/Aimin Tang; p. 15 Image courtesy of Earth Sciences and Image Analysis Laboratory, NASA Johnson Space Center.

Library of Congress Cataloging-in-Publication Data

Mis, Melody S.
    Exploring peninsulas / Melody S. Mis. — 1st ed.
        p. cm. — (Geography zone: landforms)
    Includes index.
    ISBN 978-1-4358-2711-0 (library binding) — ISBN 978-1-4358-3109-4 (pbk.)
ISBN 978-1-4358-3115-5 (6-pack)
    1. Peninsulas—Juvenile literature. I. Title.
    GB454.P46M57 2009
    551.41—dc22
                                    2008023812

Manufactured in the United States of America

Contents

A peninsula is a piece of land that has water on three sides of it. The fourth side of a peninsula is **connected** to a larger piece of land. Some peninsulas are found in oceans. Others are found in lakes. Did you know that Florida is a peninsula? It is bordered by the Atlantic Ocean and the Gulf of Mexico.

Peninsulas often have strange shapes. Italy is a peninsula that is shaped like a lady's boot. A peninsula in Michigan is shaped like the thumb of a mitten.

There is a lot more to learn about peninsulas. Let's take a look!

This is a peninsula in South Carolina. The eastern coast of the United States has many small peninsulas that reach out into the Atlantic Ocean.

Peninsulas are formed in interesting ways. Large **glaciers** form some peninsulas. Other peninsulas are formed by **volcanoes**. Sometimes, huge pieces of Earth break **apart** and form peninsulas. You can also find peninsulas that are made from sand at the end of a river or in lakes and oceans.

It takes a very long time for a peninsula to take shape. The Cape Cod peninsula, in Massachusetts, took about 5,000 years to form. Ocean waves formed Cape Cod into the shape of a bent arm. However, a large glacier, called the Laurentide Ice Sheet, first made the peninsula.

Ocean waves push soil and rock from the shore to the tip of the Cape Cod peninsula, shown here. This gives the tip its bent shape.

Glaciers form many peninsulas on Earth. A glacier is a large mass of ice. Glaciers are generally found on high mountains and in very cold parts of the world, such as the Arctic and Antarctica.

Sometimes, a glacier will move. As it moves, it picks up rocks and soil. When a glacier stops moving near a coast, the glacier then dumps the rocks and soil it has gathered. The rocks and soil can build up over time to become a peninsula.

Glaciers helped form the Antarctic Peninsula. This peninsula is the northernmost point of Antarctica.

As this glacier slowly reaches the lake, it will dump rock and soil into the water. The rock and soil could pile up and become a peninsula.

Volcanoes form many peninsulas as well. A volcano is a mountain that has **lava** inside it. When lava gets too hot, it is pushed up through the mountain. The lava causes the mountain to **erupt**. When this happens, hot lava flows down the mountainside. After the lava reaches water, it cools down and becomes hard. Every time a volcano erupts, it leaves more lava to dry and harden in the water. Over time, this dried lava can build up and form a peninsula.

Volcanoes made some of Hawaii's peninsulas. In fact, Maui's two peninsulas are **dormant** volcanoes.

Haleakala, shown here, is a dormant volcano
that makes up Maui's eastern peninsula.

Another type of peninsula is a sand spit. Sand spits are peninsulas that are made from sand.

Waves in oceans, lakes, and rivers carry sand and soil from one place to another. Sometimes, the waves drop sand at the same place. If this happens many times, the piles of sand slowly build up. The piles form a new piece of land that sticks out in the water. This new land is a peninsula.

At times, the waves change direction and the sand will wash away. This loss of sand can cause a sand spit to get smaller over time.

This is Homer Spit, in Homer, Alaska.
Homer Spit is around 4.5 miles (7 km) long.

A rift peninsula is formed when pieces of Earth break apart. Earth's top **layer** is made up of large pieces of rock called plates. When plates pull away from each other, the ground breaks apart. **Millions** of years ago, a plate broke away from Mexico. This formed the Baja California peninsula.

A delta is a low **area** at one end of a river. A river carries soil and rocks as it moves along. The river drops them when it reaches the sea. The rocks and soil pile up and form a peninsula. This is how the Mississippi River delta was formed.

The Mississippi River delta, shown here, formed when the Mississippi River dropped sand and soil into the Gulf of Mexico over a long period of time.

Animal and plant life on peninsulas is plentiful. Penguins, whales, and seals live on or near the colder peninsulas. It is too cold for some plants to grow there, though. However, you can find many plants, birds, fish, bugs, and **mammals** on warmer peninsulas around the world.

The Hawaiian peninsulas are known for their tasty fruit and beautiful flowers. In fact, Hawaiians make necklaces, called leis, out of their flowers. Hawaii is also known for its special birds, such as the *'i'iwi* and *'apapane*. The most famous bird in Hawaii is the nene goose. It is the state bird.

This is a group of Gentoo penguins on the Antarctic Peninsula. Gentoo penguins feed on small fish, so it is necessary for them to live near water.

One of the best-known peninsulas is the state of Florida. Florida sits on a **plateau**, and it was underwater for many years. Over time, the ocean pushed sand and soil onto the plateau. This made the plateau bigger, and the peninsula rose above the water. At one time, Florida was three times larger than it is now. It got smaller when the sea rose and covered some of it.

Florida is a good place to grow flowers and fruit trees. Much of our fruit comes from Florida. There are lots of snakes, bugs, and birds in Florida as well.

Miami, shown here, is a city on the southeastern tip of Florida. Because of Miami's warm weather and water, it is a common place for people to visit.

The largest peninsula on Earth is the Arabian Peninsula. It is bordered on three sides by the Red Sea, Arabian Sea, Gulf of Aden, Persian Gulf, and the Gulf of Oman. Millions of years ago, the land broke away from Africa and became a peninsula. It is very hot and dry. Most of the peninsula is desert.

Today, there are five countries on the Arabian Peninsula. They are Saudi Arabia, Yemen, Oman, Qatar, and the United Arab Emirates. Some of these countries are very important to the world because a lot of oil is found there.

The Arabian Peninsula, shown here, covers a space of around 1.2 million square miles (3 million sq km).

Many people spend time on warm peninsulas so they can be close to the water. Swimming, boating, and fishing are common activities on peninsulas. Some people live and work on peninsulas all year long, and others just go there for vacation. No one lives on the Antarctic Peninsula, though. It is too cold to enjoy any activities there.

Peninsulas are some of Earth's most interesting and beautiful landforms. There are many around the world. There might be a peninsula near your house, or maybe you will visit one. If you do, take a look around and you can learn even more!

Glossary

apart (uh-PAHRT) In or into parts or pieces.

area (ER-ee-uh) A certain space or place.

connected (kuh-NEKT-ed) Tied to or having to do with something else.

dormant (DOR-ment) Resting, not active.

erupt (ih-RUPT) To break open.

glaciers (GLAY-shurz) Large masses of ice that move down a mountain or along a valley.

lava (LAH-vuh) Hot, melted rock that comes out of a volcano.

layer (LAY-er) One thickness of something.

mammals (MA-mulz) Warm-blooded animals that have backbones and hair, breathe air, and feed milk to their young.

millions (MIL-yunz) Very large numbers.

plateau (pla-TOH) A wide, flat, high piece of land.

volcanoes (vol-KAY-nohz) Openings that sometimes shoot up hot, melted rock called lava.

Index

A

Antarctic Peninsula, 8
Arabian Peninsula, 20
area, 14
Atlantic Ocean, 4

B

Baja California, 14

C

Cape Cod, 6

F

Florida, 4, 18

G

glaciers, 6, 8
Gulf of Mexico, 4

H

Hawaii, 10, 16
Hawaiian peninsulas, 16

I

Italy, 4

L

Laurentide Ice Sheet, 6
lava, 10

M

Mississippi River delta,
  14

P

Persian Gulf, 20
plateau, 18

S

sand spit, 12
Saudi Arabia, 20

V

volcanoes, 6, 10

Web Sites

Due to the changing nature of Internet links, PowerKids Press has developed an online list of Web sites related to the subject of this book. This site is updated regularly. Please use this link to access the list:
www.powerkidslinks.com/gzone/peninsula/

ML   6/09